DEC 3 1 2014

W9-DJA-611

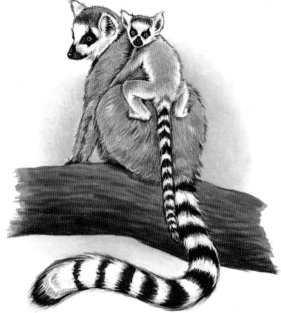

learn to draw

ANIMALS

**Learn to draw and color 26 wild
creatures, step by easy step,
shape by simple shape!**

Illustrated by Diana Fisher

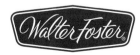

GETTING STARTED

When you look closely at the drawings in this book, you'll notice that they're made up of basic shapes, such as circles, triangles, and rectangles. To draw all your wild kingdom favorites, just start with simple shapes as you see here. It's easy and fun!

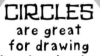 **CIRCLES** are great for drawing heads, chests, and hips.

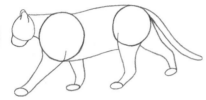 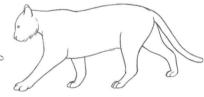

OVALS are good for drawing animals' bodies.

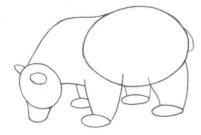 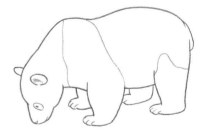

TRIANGLES are often best for drawing beaks, ears, and hooves.

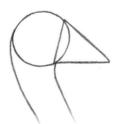 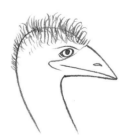

COLORING TIPS

There's more than one way to bring your animal pals to life on paper—you can use crayons, markers, or colored pencils. Just be sure you have plenty of good natural colors—black, brown, and gray, plus yellow, orange, red, and green.

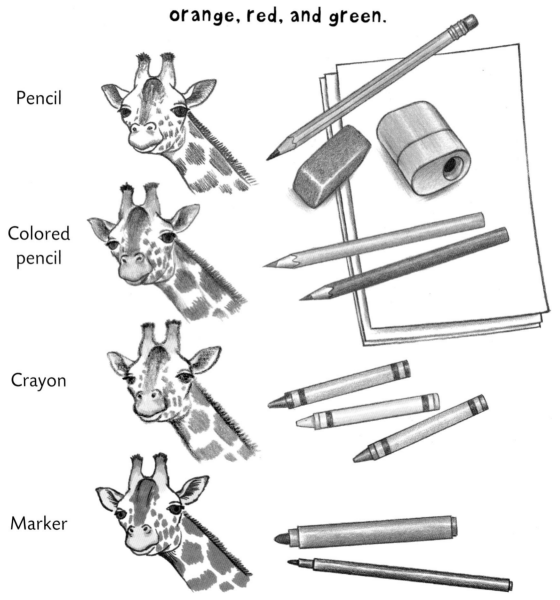

Pencil

Colored pencil

Crayon

Marker

AARDVARK

The aardvark has a long nose, sharp claws, and small, beady eyes. It first smells and then digs out its meals of ants and termites.

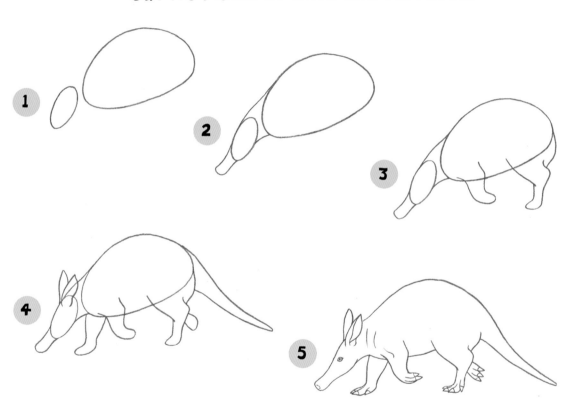

1
2
3
4
5

6

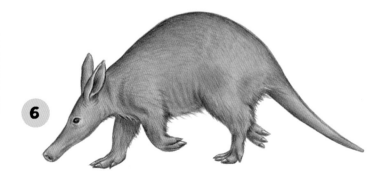

EMU

The emu's fluffy plumage hides its small wings. But its tall, thin legs allow this flightless bird to run up to 30 miles per hour!

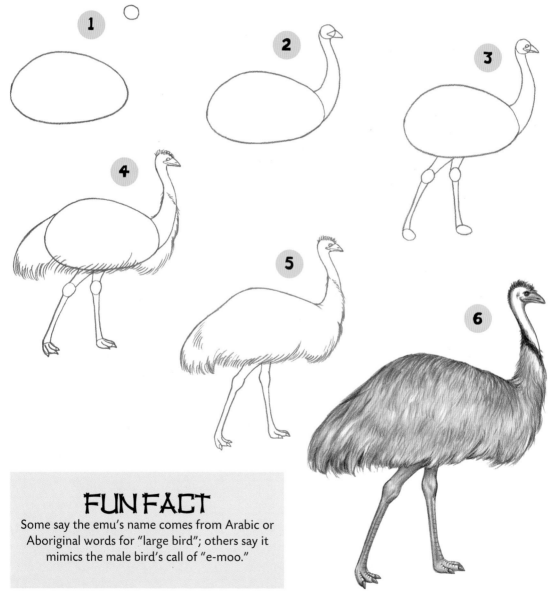

FUN FACT

Some say the emu's name comes from Arabic or Aboriginal words for "large bird"; others say it mimics the male bird's call of "e-moo."

GIANT PANDA

In china the barrel-shaped panda is called "baixiong" ("white bear"), but the black markings give this animal a two-toned look.

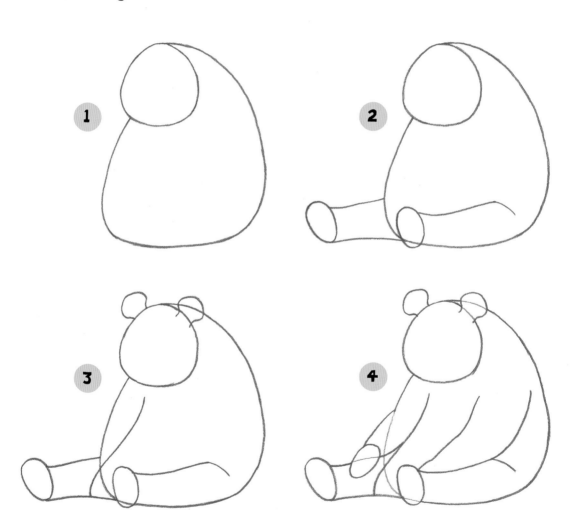

FUN FACT

The giant panda has a very limited diet—it survives almost entirely on bamboo! It eats the shoots of this grasslike plant in the spring, leaves in the summer, and stems in the winter.

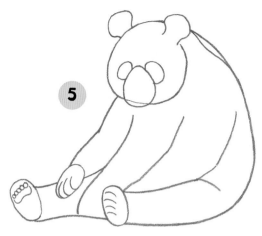

5

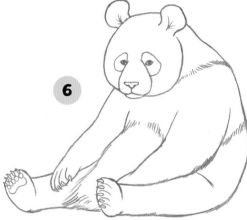

6

High Risk

The panda is at high risk for extinction; its kind (or species) is endangered. There are very few giant pandas alive in the wild today.

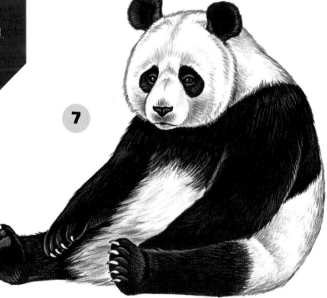

7

POLAR BEAR

The cuddly-looking polar bear has a large,
round, furry body—but this cutie hunts and devours
seals, walruses, and even whales!

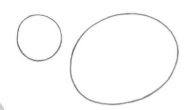

1

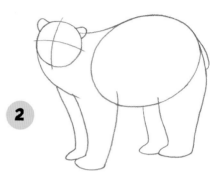

2

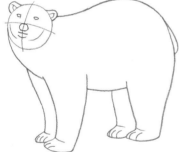
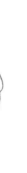

3

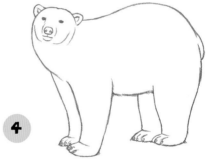

4

At Risk

The population of polar
bears decreases every
day. Efforts must be made
to save the bear and its Arctic
home to prevent extinction.

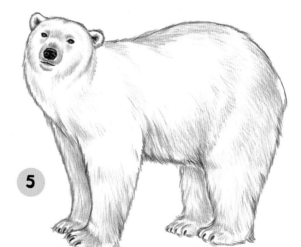

5

CHEETAH

with its long, powerful legs; lean, muscular body; and stylish, spotted coat, you might say the cheetah is a hunter "dressed to kill"!

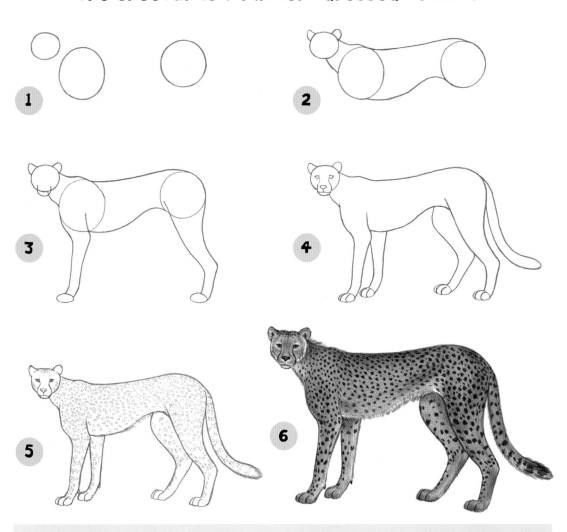

FUN FACT

Sure, the cheetah is quick—it can reach speeds of more than 60 mph, making it the fastest animal in the world. But this big cat can maintain its top speed only for short bursts. After 10–12 seconds of running, the cheetah begins to overheat.

High Risk

ELEPHANT

One of the largest beasts of the animal kingdom, an African elephant has a thick trunk, big legs, long tusks, and giant ears!

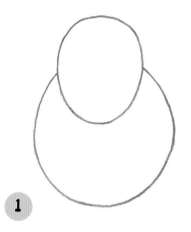

1

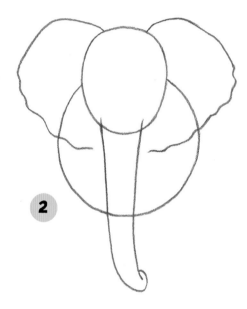

2

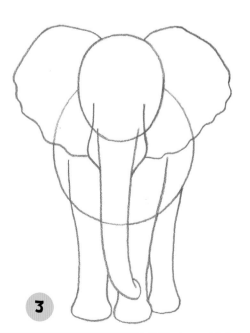

3

FUN FACT

The elephant is known for its great memory—but why? One reason is the elephant has an enormous brain! Weighing in at around 12 pounds, it's the largest and heaviest mammal brain. (The human brain weighs only about 3 pounds.)

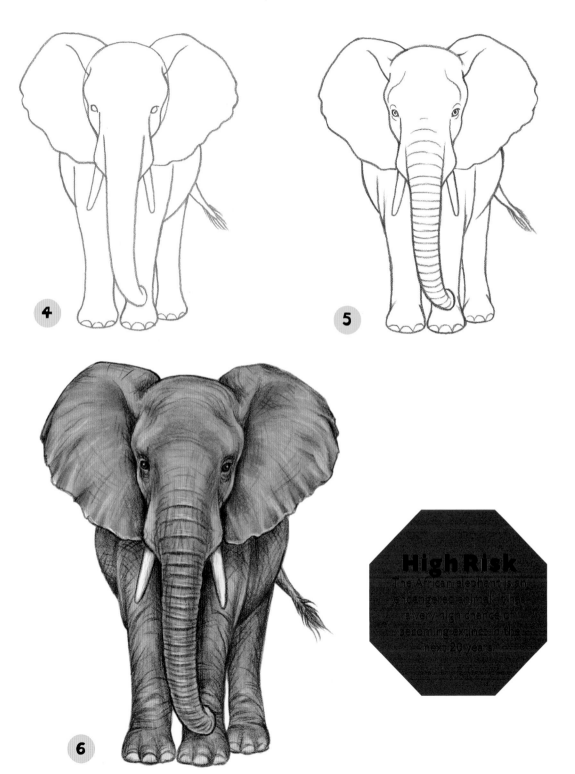

High Risk
The African elephant is an
endangered animal. It has
a very high chance of
becoming extinct in the
next 20 years.

TIGER

Every big cat has a large head and rounded ears.
But a tiger also has camouflaging stripes
that help this stand-out cat blend in!

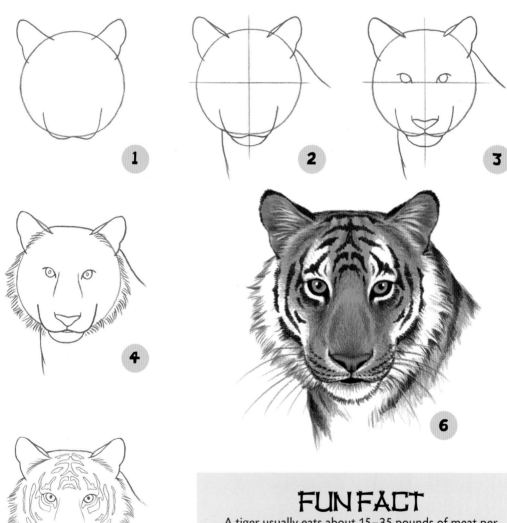

1

2

3

4

5

6

FUN FACT

A tiger usually eats about 15–35 pounds of meat per feeding, dining on deer, pigs, cattle, monkeys, birds, reptiles, and even fish. And when it's really hungry, a tiger can eat up to 90 pounds of meat in one meal!

TOUCAN

It's hard to ignore the keel-billed toucan's beak!
It's almost as long as the bird's body—
and it features a rainbow of colors.

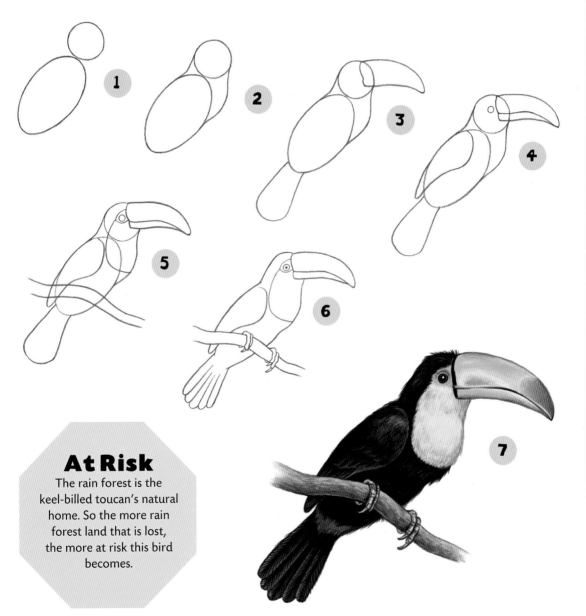

At Risk

The rain forest is the keel-billed toucan's natural home. So the more rain forest land that is lost, the more at risk this bird becomes.

13

GIRAFFE

with its lanky legs and long neck, the towering giraffe rises above the competition to claim the title of "tallest animal on Earth."

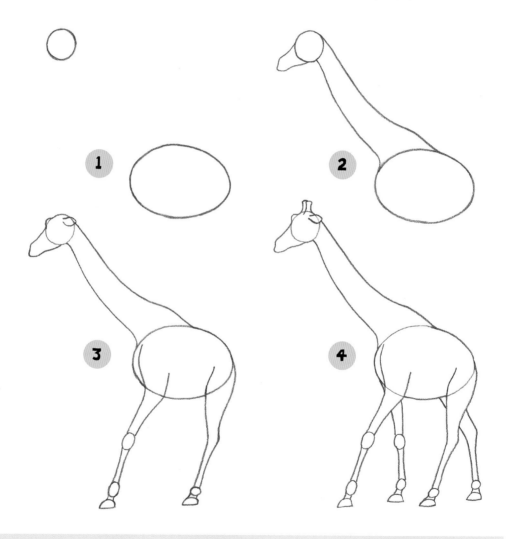

FUN FACT

A baby giraffe, called a "calf," can stand up on its own about 20 minutes after it's born! And, at birth, a giraffe calf already measures about 6-1/2 feet tall!

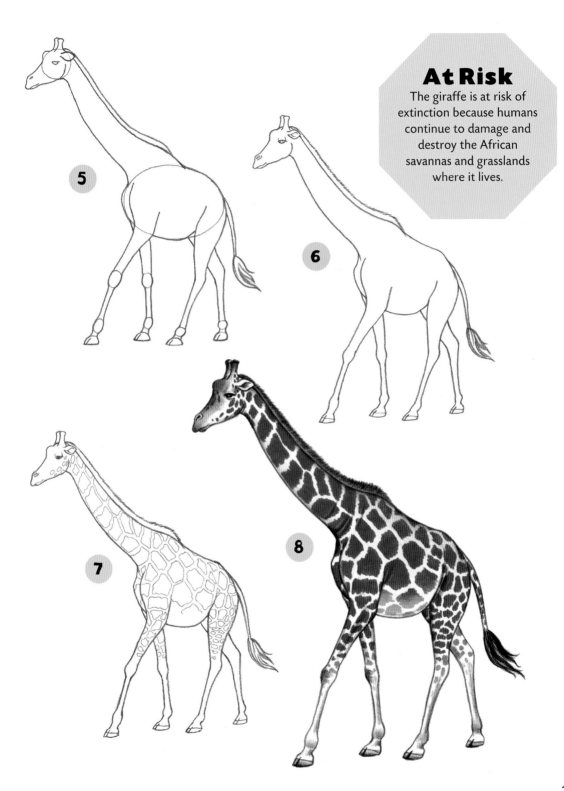

At Risk

The giraffe is at risk of extinction because humans continue to damage and destroy the African savannas and grasslands where it lives.

5

6

7

8

15

WILDEBEEST

The wildebeest—or gnu—looks big and broad with high shoulders and a humped back, but it prances away from danger on four skinny legs!

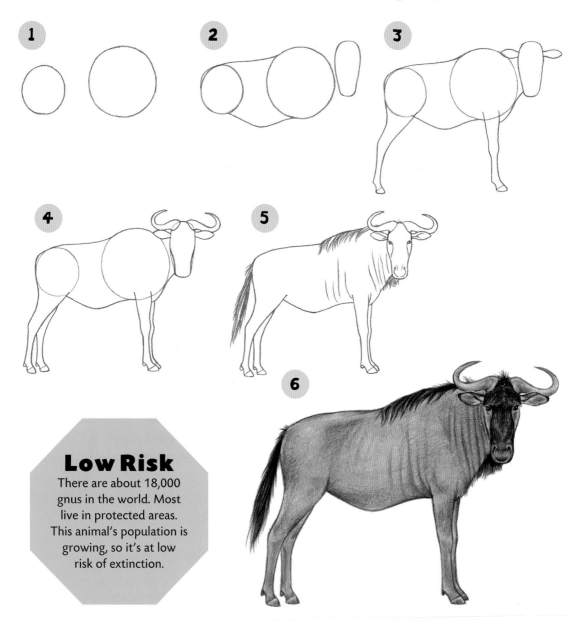

CROCODILE

Start this drawing with a thin oval body and a small round head—then add the crocodile's long, strong tail and big, powerful jaws!

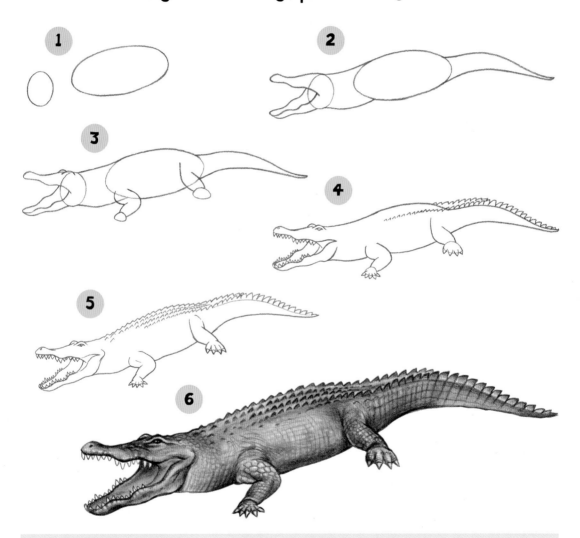

FUN FACT

Can't tell the difference between the crocodile and the alligator? Check out the snout. The crocodile's snout is longer and V-shaped; the alligator's snout is wider and U-shaped.

17

HIPPOPOTAMUS

"Massive" is a good start for
describing this round, hulking beast!
A full-grown hippo can weigh up to 1-1/2 tons.

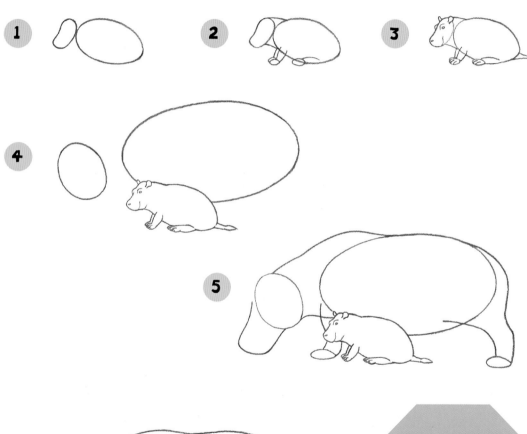

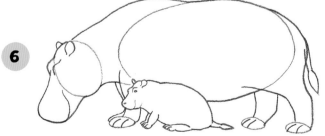

Low Risk

The hippopotamus is
plentiful in the African wild.
Its population numbers are
steady, so it has a low
risk of becoming
extinct.

18

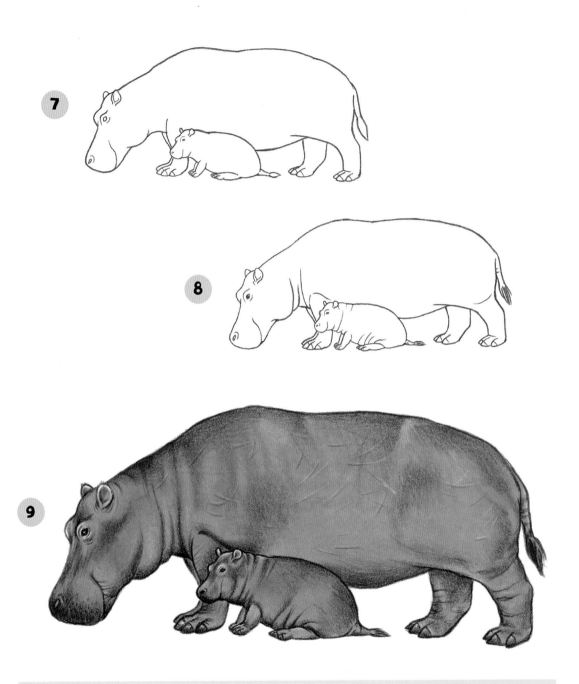

FUN FACT

The common hippo is amphibious, meaning it lives both on land and in water. Its webbed toes and high-placed eyes, ears, and nostrils allow it to easily take a breath, a look, and a listen while spending long periods of time underwater.

ANIMALS IN THE WILD

Each animal has a natural environment, or habitat—whether a desert, forest, or water. To realistically portray your favorite animals, draw them in their own wild habitat, like this African grassland!

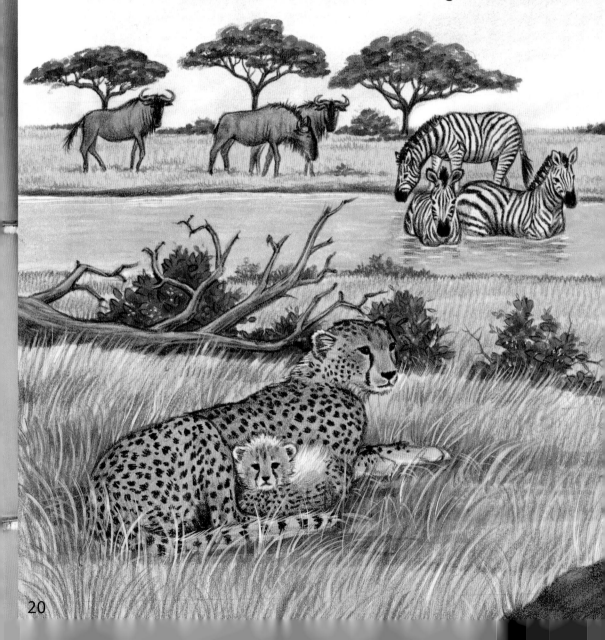

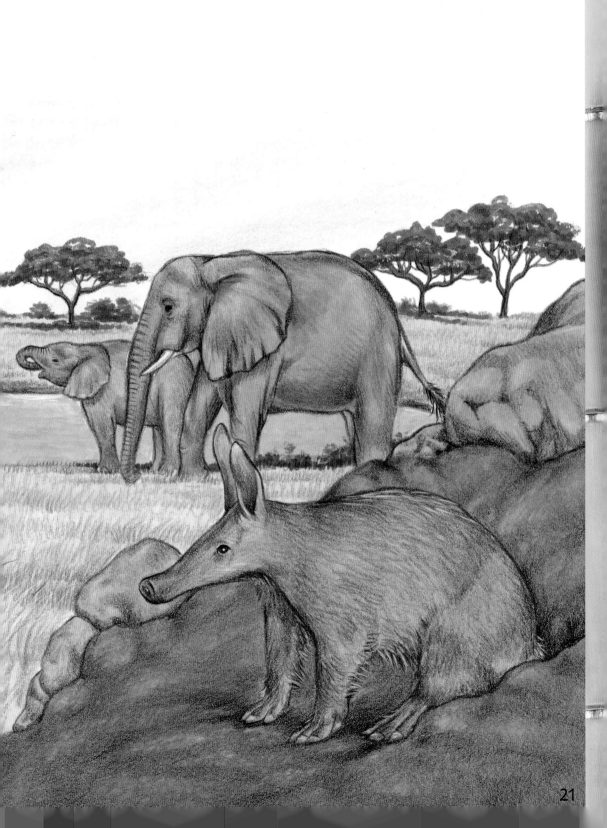

KANGAROO

with a thick, powerful tail, strong hind legs, and huge rear feet, you can identify the kangaroo from a hop, skip, and a jump away!

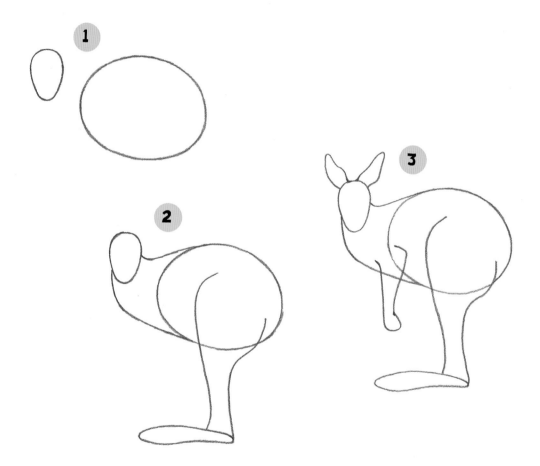

1

2

3

FUN FACT

For male kangaroos, kick boxing isn't a sport; it's a way of life. When fighting over mates, food, and resting spots, kangaroos will lock arms with each other, lean on their tails, and kick. The first kangaroo to get pushed over loses.

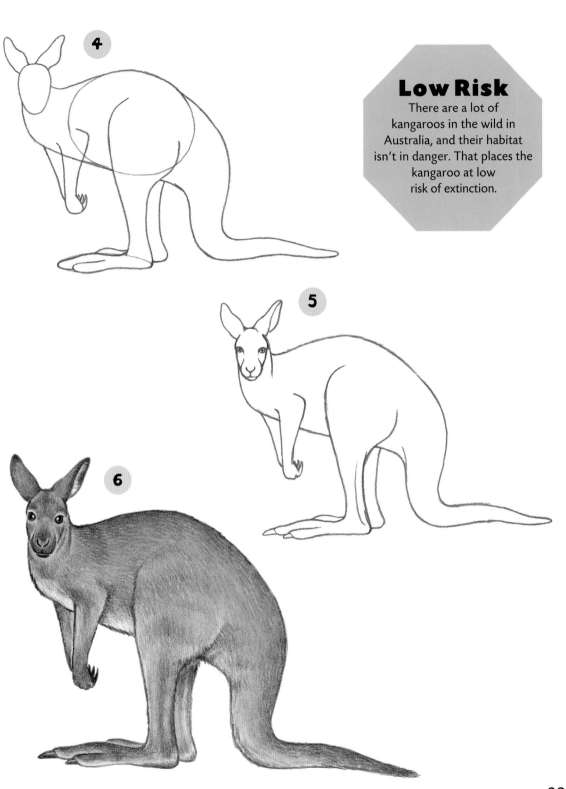

23

KOALA

This soft, woolly tree-dweller suspends its short, round body by clinging to eucalyptus trees—both its home and its food.

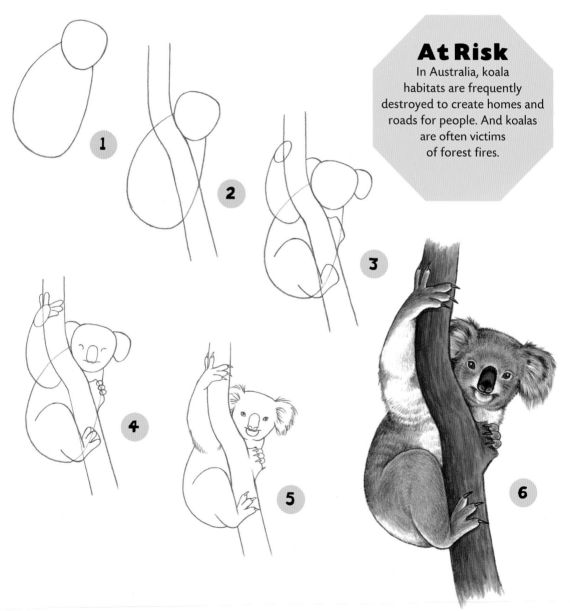

24

LEMUR

Although its long, curving tail is the ring-tailed lemur's most striking feature, this animal is also known for its graceful, catlike posture.

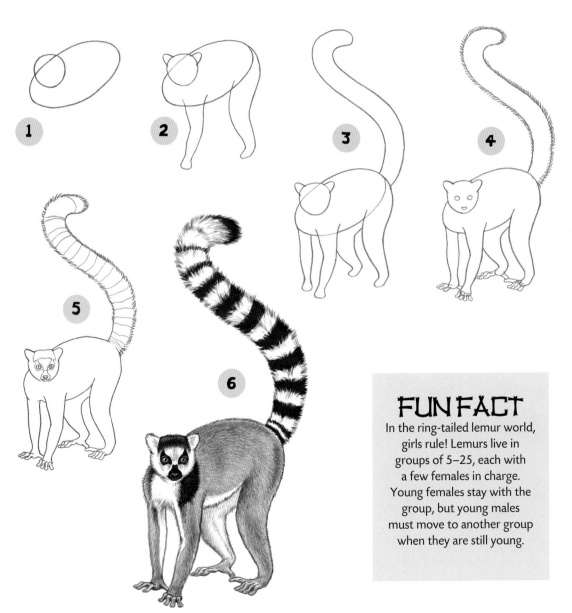

FUN FACT

In the ring-tailed lemur world, girls rule! Lemurs live in groups of 5–25, each with a few females in charge. Young females stay with the group, but young males must move to another group when they are still young.

SPIDER MONKEY

Black-handed spider monkeys are small and thin. Their hands, feet, and heads are black, and black masks frame their round eyes.

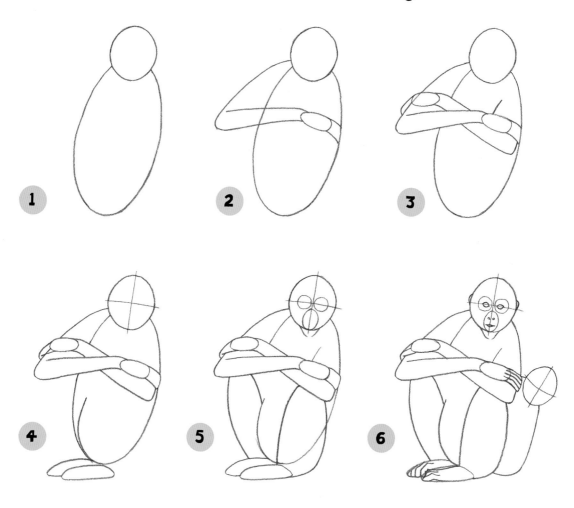

1   2   3
4   5   6

FUN FACT

This monkey gets its name from its long, spidery limbs—all five of them! The spider monkey's tail is as long and as strong as its arms and legs. And the tail's hairless tip makes it easier for the monkey to tightly grasp branches or food!

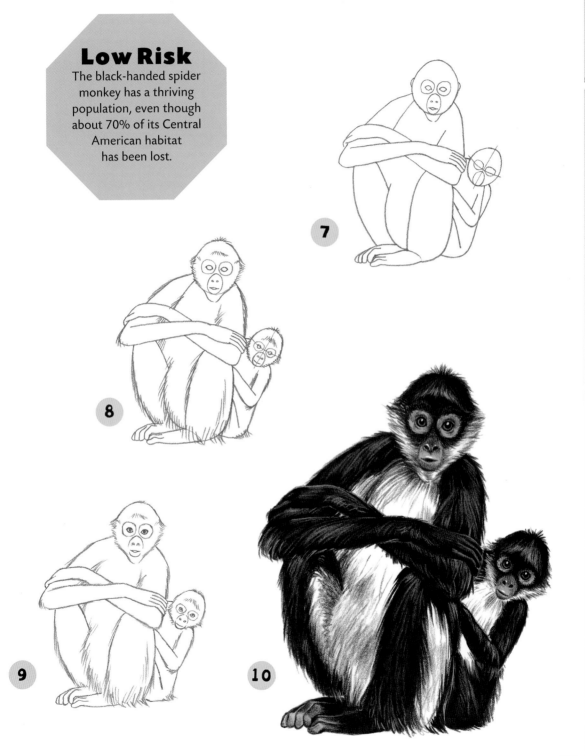

Low Risk

The black-handed spider monkey has a thriving population, even though about 70% of its Central American habitat has been lost.

7

8

9

10

27

KOMODO DRAGON

Don't let its draggin' belly fool you—the large, wrinkled, prehistoric-looking Komodo dragon is a swift runner and a fast climber.

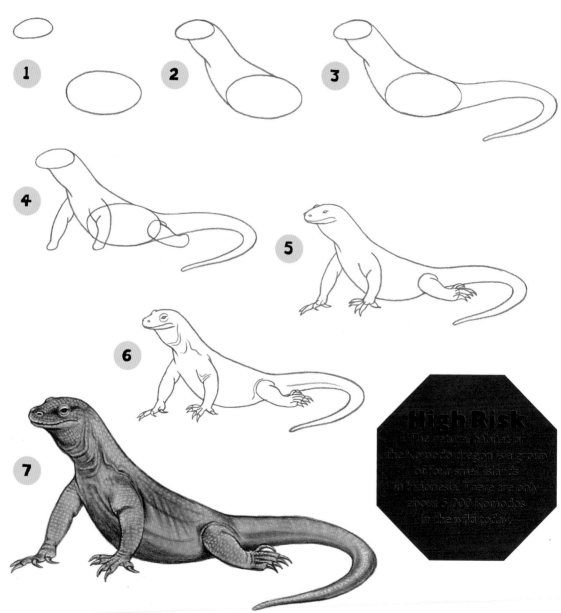

1

2

3

4

5

6

7

ARMADILLO

Low Risk

Oddly enough, the "nine-banded" armadillo can have from 8 to 10 bands around its body, making its tough armor more flexible.

1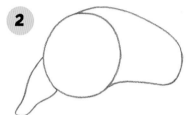

2

3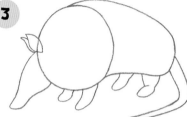

4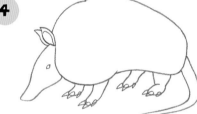

FUN FACT

Many mammals give birth to multiple young, but only the nine-banded armadillo regularly produces them all from a single egg. The female nine-banded armadillo always gives birth to quadruplets—that's four identical baby armadillos.

5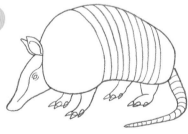

6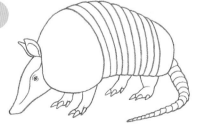

7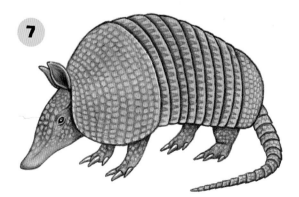

RHINOCEROS

The short legs of this white rhino support its bulky body, and it uses its two curved, triangular-shaped horns to dig food and defend itself!

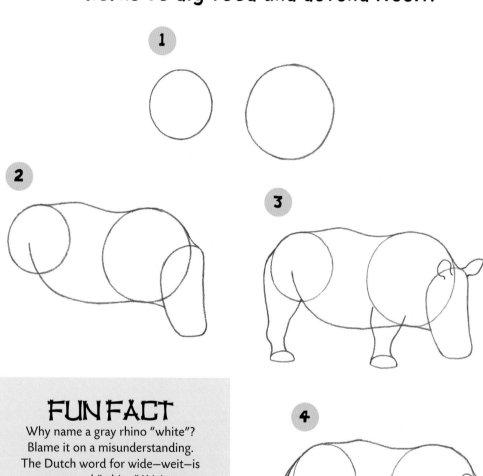

1

2

3

FUN FACT

Why name a gray rhino "white"? Blame it on a misunderstanding. The Dutch word for wide—weit—is pronounced "white." Weit was meant to describe the rhino's wide, square muzzle—not its color. It's no coincidence that this animal is also called the "square-lipped" rhino.

4

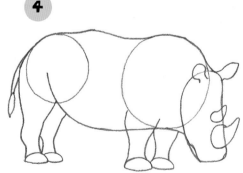

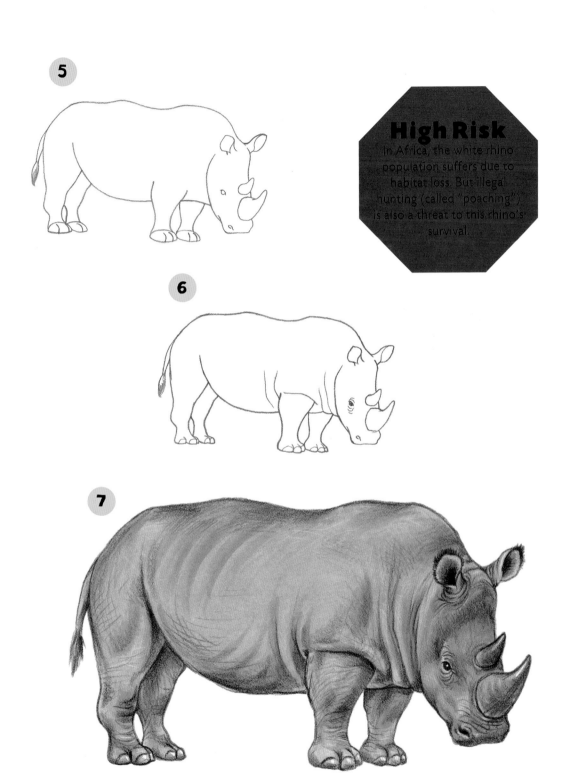

5

6

7

31

High Risk

In Africa, the white rhino population suffers due to habitat loss. But illegal hunting (called "poaching") is also a threat to this rhino's survival.

PLATYPUS

It may have a duck's bill and webbed feet, but the platypus's flat tail and velvety, waterproof coat are all its own!

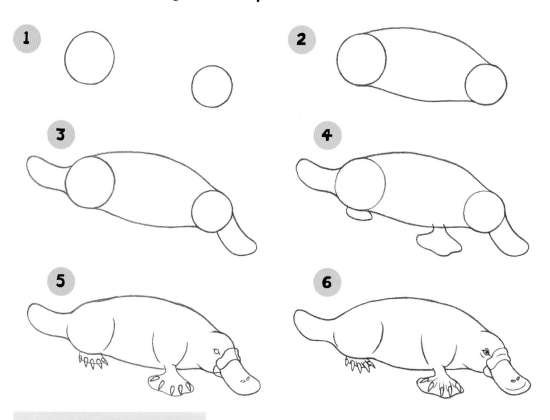

1 **2** **3** **4** **5** **6**

FUN FACT

The platypus isn't psychic, but it does have ESP—extra sensory perception! In addition to using sight, sound, taste, smell, and touch, the platypus can sense tiny electrical signals with its snout, helping it find food underwater.

7

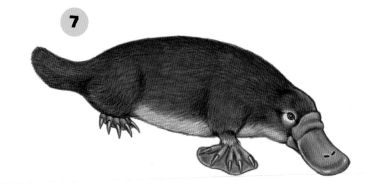

ORANGUTAN

Every orangutan has a bare face,
round eyes, and small ears, but only the male has
large, round cheek pads and a long, hairy beard.

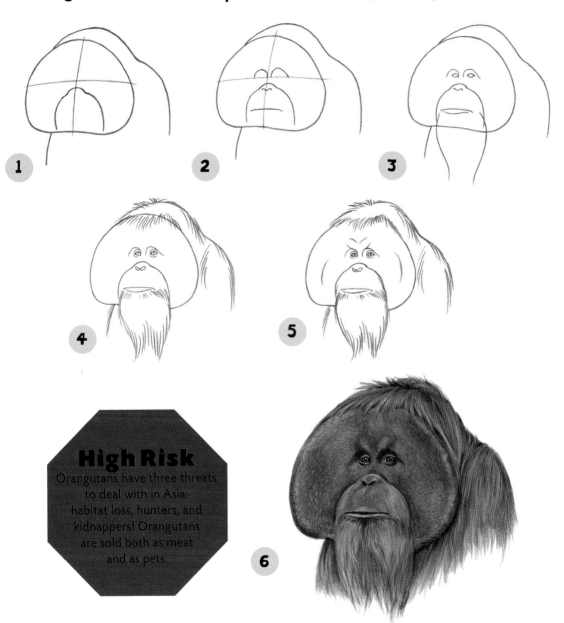

High Risk

Orangutans have three threats
to deal with in Asia:
habitat loss, hunters, and
kidnappers! Orangutans
are sold both as meat
and as pets.

TAPIR

what's black and white with a long curved snout?
The Malayan tapir! This "living fossil" has looked
exactly the same for 30 million years!

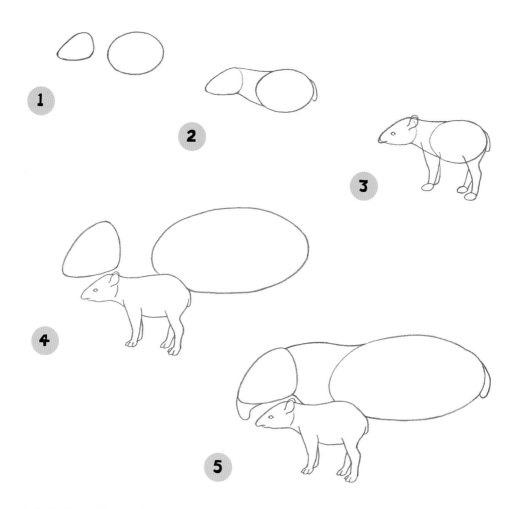

FUN FACT

Every tapir is born with spots and stripes. This camouflage
pattern protects the young tapir from predators, helping it
blend in with vegetation. The "broken" coloration of the adult
Malayan tapir also acts as camouflage.

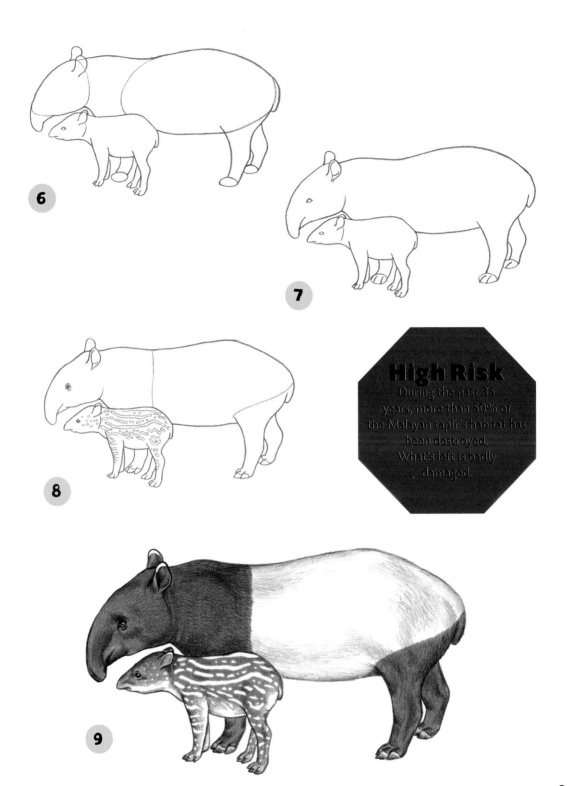

6

7

8

High Risk

During the past 35 years, more than 50% of the Malayan tapir's habitat has been destroyed. What's left is badly damaged.

9

HYENA

The spotted hyena has many doglike features, but its large, rounded ears and sloping back give this animal a unique appearance.

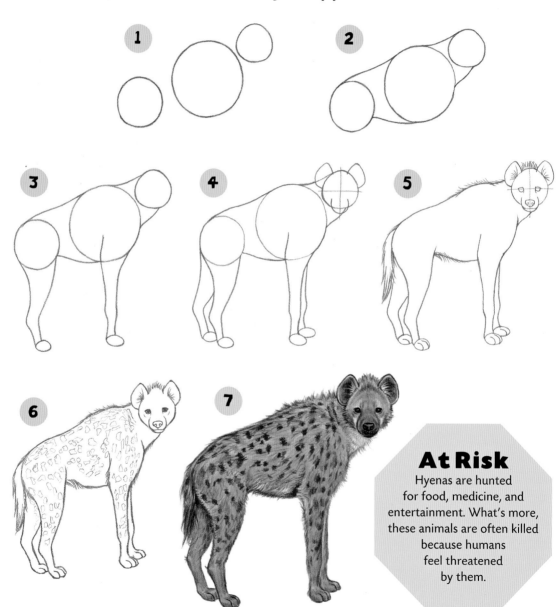

At Risk

Hyenas are hunted for food, medicine, and entertainment. What's more, these animals are often killed because humans feel threatened by them.

WOMBAT

Featuring a compact body, stocky limbs, and a pointed snout, the wombat looks kind of like a small bear crossed with a pig!

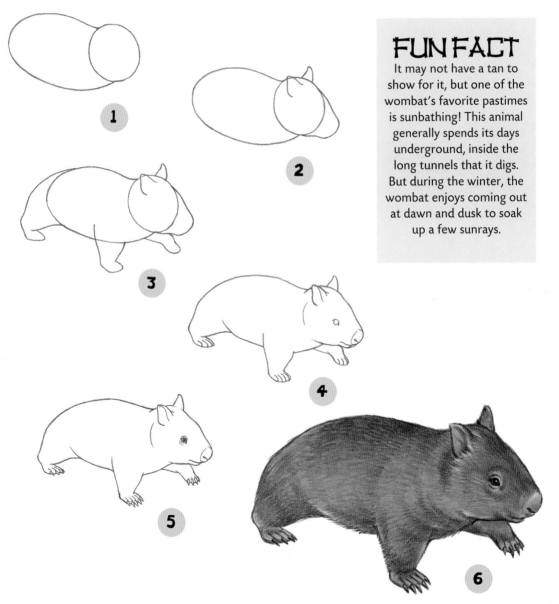

FUN FACT

It may not have a tan to show for it, but one of the wombat's favorite pastimes is sunbathing! This animal generally spends its days underground, inside the long tunnels that it digs. But during the winter, the wombat enjoys coming out at dawn and dusk to soak up a few sunrays.

OKAPI

Its stripes make the okapi look like a zebra, but this tall, two-toned animal has the long legs and flexible neck of a giraffe.

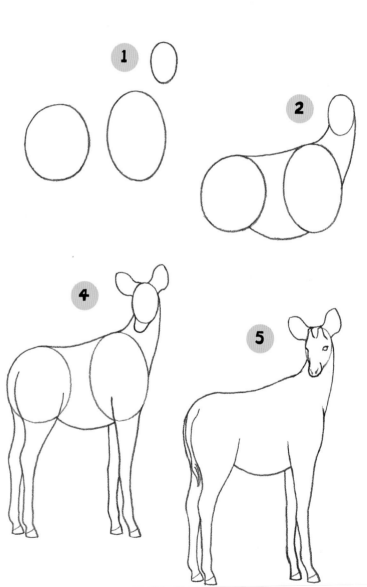

38

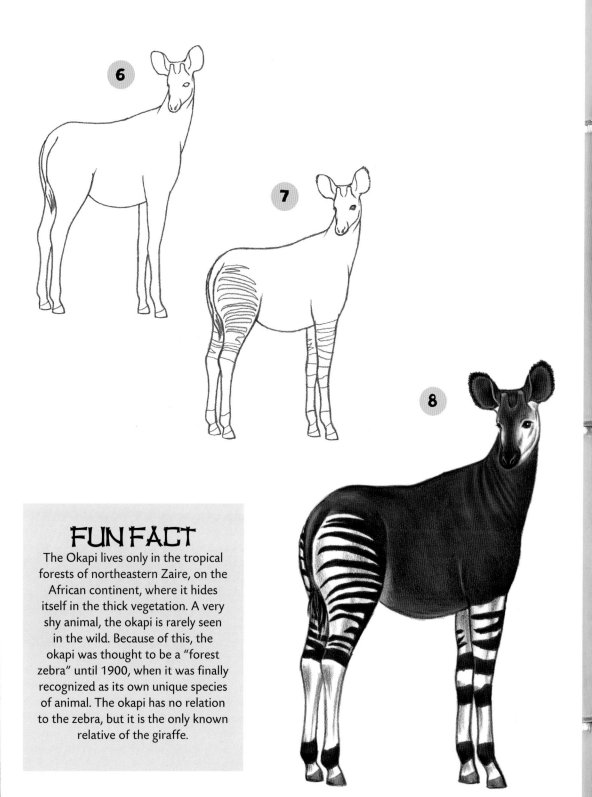

FUN FACT

The Okapi lives only in the tropical forests of northeastern Zaire, on the African continent, where it hides itself in the thick vegetation. A very shy animal, the okapi is rarely seen in the wild. Because of this, the okapi was thought to be a "forest zebra" until 1900, when it was finally recognized as its own unique species of animal. The okapi has no relation to the zebra, but it is the only known relative of the giraffe.

ZEBRA

From its black muzzle to the tips of its long ears, the zebra's face is covered in narrow stripes; its body and mane have broader stripes.

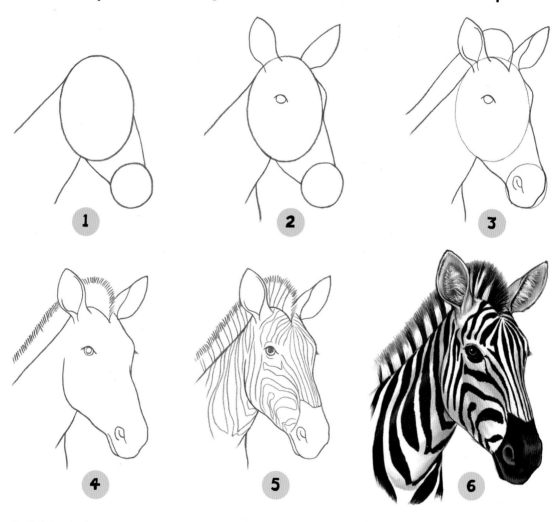

FUN FACT

Experts aren't exactly sure why zebras have stripes, but they think that the markings serve some sort of purpose. The stripes might help the animals recognize other members of their herd, regulate temperature, or even confuse predators.